Wait for Me
in the Rainbow

Laura Vidal

Wait for Me in the Rainbow - Laura Vidal
Original title: *Espérame en el arcoíris*, 2019
© *2022, Laura Vidal*
© *2022 for this translation*

First edition: December 2022

Translated by Georgia Delena
Editorial layout: Georgia Delena
Cover design: Sara García
www.maquetacionlibros.com

What readers think of the book on Amazon.es

SOME ALEATORY REVIEWS:

☛ "Hope, light and a lot of understanding.

A book that is a balm for understanding the process of the animal owner, evaluating in life and resignifying the death of our furry."

☛ "I really liked the book. It has helped me to confirm my feelings towards animals and to prepare myself once again for when I have to walk through that labyrinth. I have no doubt that we will see each other when we pass the rainbow bridge."

☛ "Good book, it has helped me overcome the death of my dog, at first I could only read 3 pages and I cried so much, but while I was reading the pain passed a little, it brings many recommendations to pass the mourning of our companion animals, it has helped me a lot to relieve my pain."

👉 " Amazing Book.

Helped my wife a lot! Thanks "Wait for me in the Rainbow" a book that is full of wisdom. Thank you for sharing."

👉 " A relief in pain.

If you feel deep pain because your friend left, this book, written from the heart, will give you hope.

If you still have him with you, it will help you live your time with him to the fullest."

👉 "An essential and necessary book.

Finally, a book to help you overcome animal grief. The way in which Laura transmits and excites with this book is total, and it is appreciated that she puts so many feelings in writing."

👉 " Thank you for this hug in book form.

It embraces you, understands you and accompanies you in your pain. It's a door to start relieving so much pain. Thank you Laura."

Who is Laura?

Born in Alicante, in 1984. She studied Veterinary Technical Assistance, which led her to work as an assistant in this field for many years. A great lover of animals, after losing her furry life companions, she suffered a tough grieving process that led her to take her life in another direction. She changed her way of seeing life and death and reflected her story of healing through pain in her first book "Wait for Me in the Rainbow", a bestseller translated into several languages and permanently placed at the top of sales on Amazon in the pet´s category. Her second book "Cuando ya no estás", published by the Vergara publishing house, reached its fourth edition a few months after its launch; it is a practical guide to face the mourning for the animals with which we live.

As a result of her success, Laura took great advantage of her personal experience to find her life mission: to help others grieve the loss of their animals. Apart from writing, Laura currently accompanies animal mourning, online courses, gives workshops, talks and interviews about the pain of losing the furry members of the house. It also helps many people find their purpose in life through self-improvement.

Index

Introduction

Currently, at a global level, more and more humans are taking into consideration animals in general, but especially those who share a home and life with us. This is so to such an extent that for many of us our furry companions have become one more member of the family, with full rights; we take them to the vet when they have health problems, we enjoy activities with them, we prepare our house and our routines for their well-being, we choose vacations in places where they are accepted or we pay the extra to leave them in a good hotel or with a good babysitter, we fill our mobile phones and our social networks with their photos, we buy them gifts for Christmas, they are the first ones we greet when we get home and many of them, even, sleep in the bed of a family member; we love them with all our heart and they are an indispensable part of our home.

According to a study concluded by the Affinity Foundation together with AVEPA[1], carried out on a base of more than 4000 people who lived with dogs, two different groups of owners have been identified in relation to the characteristics of the bonding pattern.

- The first group, which we call "emotional", represents 75% of our population. It is characterized by a relationship where the emotional bond with the dog is very intense. For these people, their dog is a very important source of emotional support, especially in difficult situations.

- The second group, which we have called "pragmatic", represents the remaining 25% of the population studied. For them, living with a dog brings benefits, but the emotional dimension is not so intense.

A curious fact in the evaluation is that, in children, the affinity with animals is a majority phenomenon. This result would agree with the hypothesis that curiosity and affinity for nature and for living beings is a universal human trait.

Despite the fact that, as we see, we form a very strong bond with the animals we live with, we have to deal with a painful and inevitable truth. The life cycle of animals is shorter than ours, so in the vast majority of cases we will

---

[1] Spanish Small Animal Veterinary Association.

survive many of our companions. This is very hard to take in, I know... but what happens when the dreaded moment arrives? Here we are faced with a dichotomy: what one feels about it and what is politically correct.

How many people have been given a day off at work for the death of their furry?

How many have been able to openly cry in front of family and friends at this fact?

How many have looked for a professional to help them get through their grief without feeling embarrassed?

How many of us have prepared ourselves for this dreaded moment?

Yes, there are many of us who have gone through the same situation and we have found ourselves without having anyone to turn to, ashamed and hiding our pain, since it seems that it´s not yet socially accepted for a person to go through a process of grief and mourning for an animal. There are practically not even books written in Spanish on this subject, so here is my contribution to all of us who have little marks on our hearts. This book will help you prepare for the departure of your partner or help you overcome it, walking the path with you so that you can develop a proper mourning.

My personal experience helped me realize that I did not want any other person to feel as lonely and lost as I felt in those hard times, so I ended up making my pain my profession and after training in coaching and counselling, I live for and to help people to develop a good mourning for their furry, on the basis of understanding, support and respect.

I invite you to read this book from the soul, although it´s a very personal subject, since each of us reacts to pain and loss in a different way. I invite you to prioritize the parts of the book that may be helpful to you and to let go of what doesn't resonate with you.

This book is for you and me.

"Grief is the price we pay for love".

(E.A. Bucchianeri)

1. The worst dog in the world

As an animal lover, the truth is that I have spent my whole life sharing it with dogs, cats and even with a parrot. I have been able to enjoy different colleagues who have taught me different things, with whom I´ve lived many unforgettable moments; and, if I'm honest, for me life is fuller accompanied by one of these four-legged furry friends.

My first dog was named Kira and she is probably the one to blame for my love for animals. I think all I'm trying to do is give back to her kind a little bit of what she gave me. While sharing my life with Kira, we also had King and Gala, two noble and loving bobtails, very handsome, very good, very funny but... not very "smart".

Later I became independent and with that I fulfilled the illusion of having the first dog that was only mine, my dog, as I called him, and the truth, with all the affection that a mother feels for her son, I can say that he was the worst dog in the world.

Galo was a German Bulldog. I close my eyes and I can still remember the first time I saw one: I was amazed, my eyes wide, I couldn't take my eyes off that being so majestic, so perfect, they call him the Apollo of dogs and understandably, it was so elegant and big that I fell in love.

It was a breed that I loved from my earliest childhood, because I have always been a Scooby-Doo super fan, but I had never seen one in person. That's why, from that first time, I felt a crush and I knew that I wanted to put a bulldog in my life; but of course, the first thing I did was start researching everything I could about the breed and I showed it to my mother, who was horrified to see this mix between pony and dog, and told me not to even dare to think that she was going to allow that animal in her house;

Galo as a baby, his first photo

so the only thing I could do for years was read about them, see photos and videos and continue like this until it was time to become independent. I fulfilled my dream and had no doubts when choosing my first dog, Galo; and yes, I bought it from a good breeder, because at that time I did not know a lot about animal adoption.

They sent me a photo of Galo, he was a baby that could fit in the palm of my hand, but until he had all the vaccinations given, they did not give me permission to go and pick him up. I remember that August 10th when, together with two other friends, we drove to get him. I was so excited that as soon as I saw it, I started to cry. Later we went all together to the mall where we bought him little food, his bed and a carrot, which would become his favorite toy for many years. I remember the illusion and that longing for his love; I wanted him to love me, to know that I was his mother and that I would love and care for him forever. How nice everything, right?! I still didn't know anything about what awaited me ahead. That little one began to grow by leaps and bounds, but it did not grow all at once like normal dogs, it seemed that it was developing in pieces. Suddenly, it had legs that were out of proportion to the head; a couple of weeks later, the head was gigantic compared to the body... I decided to take a few days off so I could be with him in his first days at home and see how he adjusted.

At that time, I was sharing a flat with a friend. Before I went back to work, my friend recommended that we should just leave him alone at home for a little while, so that he could get used to it and see how he was behaving, so we decided to go out and sit on the stairs for a while. While we waited, we thought about what Galo would be doing. After about 15/20 minutes we entered the house. It was all quiet and we thought he must have fallen asleep, until we entered the living room. The image that appeared before me was grotesque; Galo was lying on the sofa and between his legs was the sewing kit that he had managed to open and dug inside: it was completely full of needles and threads. We freeze, I told my friend not to make any sudden movements and that we would get closer little by little, trying to stay calm so that Galo wouldn´t move around the sofa full of pins. It only took 10 minutes and we were already in the car, on the way to the vet, in case he had swallowed a needle. They did some X-rays and they sent us home because he was fine… and that had been the first 15 minutes alone. From then on, we could say that everything went downhill. That was the first run to the vet on the long list we would have to do.

One day, when we returned from work, we had no sofa: half of it had literally disappeared; the next, he had eaten a piece of wall; if we took off our glasses and left them on the table to take a nap, when we woke up, he had eaten them. I was so scared for my little one, that it was all visits to the vet because I couldn't believe that a puppy would be able to eat glasses, a cell phone or things like that, without piercing his stomach, but the truth is that they suited him wonderfully.

Galo after eating the couch

Getting him used to do its business on the street, we could say that it was also an epic adventure. I remember those nights when, at 12:00 and 1:00 in the morning, I was trying to make him pee and poop; sometimes, I was so desperate that the idea of pulling down my pants and peeing in the open air so that he could see it crossed my mind, thinking that maybe he would know that that was what he had to do, not spending hours on the street, in the dark, for fun. One of those days when after I got home at 12:30 p.m., he suddenly took a giant pee (apparently, he had been holding on to do it at home). I went for the mop bucket, I poured in the water and the bleach and scrubbed the living room floor; my friend and I talked, commenting on how it was possible that he was able to hold on for so many hours during the walk and so little when he was at home, when we suddenly thought we heard a waterfall. We were silent, what was that noise? We both identified him in the same second, we looked into each other's eyes and ran away. Galo was drinking the water from the bucket where I had put the bleach... and that was our fifth visit to the vet.

I know that many dogs like food, but I have never seen another dog that will like it as much as Galo. We learned that we should never leave our food; if there was a knock on the door or a call at the home phone, we would get up with our plate of food. Our friend didn't need you to get lost for more than a second for what you had on your plate and the food to disappear; one of the most incredible things was the disappearance of a whole "toña"[2], in less than three seconds. The worst thing is that he not only tried to eat the food in our house, but when we took him out for a walk, he was a kind of vacuum cleaner whose mission was to suck up anything that seemed minimally edible to him.

---

[2] It's a dessert from Spain, from the Valencian Community. There are several varieties, the one that is consumed throughout the year is known as "pan-quemado", "toña" or "fogaseta".

I emphasize the word "seems", because many of those things were not truly edible. The worst of them was a used condom that he chewed like strawberry gum. I remember my panic in case he suffocated, mixed with the maximum disgust, and, at that moment, as I opened his mouth and reached to remove it, while crying and holding the gag, I understood the famous phrase: "A mother is capable to do anything for her son."

Galo was also a very loving dog. When we were in the car, he always tried to go as close to the front as possible. One day, they told me that I could be fined and that it was not safe to carry him loose in the car, so I bought a safety net to separate the front and back seats, where Galo was going. I laid the net with all my enthusiasm and that same Sunday my friends and I decided to go on an excursion. As Galo needed the whole back for himself, a friend took her own car, with a few more girls, and I was in my car with my friend Laura and Galo behind, who constantly pushed the net with his head, to try to touch my shoulder. Laura and I laughed a lot, seeing how affectionate he was and the desire he had to be with us, he never got tired of you touching him, he always wanted more and more and more caresses. I remember how we were driving like this in the car, laughing, when suddenly my friends who were in the car ahead, stopped. "What's going on?" we asked ourselves. A bicycle race was passing and there were some civil defense workers blocking the way. Laura and I stayed calm in the car, we weren't in a hurry, Galo was calm and we didn't mind waiting for the cycle race to pass, when suddenly I noticed something wet touching my ankles. I got really scared and I screamed; when I looked down, I couldn't believe it; Galo's half head was sticking out from under my chair and he was stretching his tongue as far as possible to get to suck my ankles, but then when he tried to go back to his seat, I realized that he couldn't, had gotten stuck under the driver's seat, with the head in the front and the body in the back. I had a panic attack when I saw my furry trapped that way. My friend was trying to calm me down. We got out of the car and told the other friends. We debated whether to disassemble the chair; if we moved it, we could squeeze him and do more damage. I got so overwhelmed that I started crying. No one could explain how he had fit in there, the only thing I can tell is that we ended up crossing the cyclist career, escorted by the local police to a veterinarian, after having argued with a poor civil protection boy who did not let us pass, to whom in that moment of stress I threatened the famous gangster style (passing my thumb around his neck), telling him that if something happened to my dog, I had memorized his face and I would come back for him.

When Galo finally became an adult, he was a beautiful giant dog, but he always had the same baby mentality, he always wanted to be in the arms of someone, even though it was practically impossible. He had a horrible panic of heights, so if he climbed any step a little higher than normal, we had to get up the courage to pick up those 80 kilos of weight and get him down of the step.

Due to life circumstances, for a few years we lived in Sardinia, Italy. Every time I went to and from home, I made the journey by car, I did not want my fearful boy to go through the stress of a trip in a winery. Surely not many people have made a 1600 km trip in a Citroën C3, with a dog glued into the back seats. I felt totally observed, people argued about whether it was a dog in the car or a cow. I suppose it would be very funny to see how my little car moved at traffic lights to the rhythm of Galo's breathing. When we arrived in Livorno, we would take the ferry that took us to the island (one of the few that allows animals to travel with their owners) and we would spend the night in the cabin, cuddled on our bed, getting dizzy together.

I loved taking my boy with me whenever I could and I used to take him when I was meeting for lunch, dinner or a drink. Of course, I made the typical mistake, I suppose as a beginner, of tying it to a table, naively thinking that he was not going to be able to move it but... he could. Table included, he ran down the sidewalk; drinks, plates, cutlery flew off the table... the worst was when he realized that he was carrying the table behind him, he got scared, so he ran more and more to try to get away from the table, but then the table was going faster and faster, which made him more scared. Catching him was a real show and thank goodness German Bulldogs are not as agile as Greyhounds, otherwise he'd still be running with a table tied up.

Galo did a lot of pranks if he was left alone for a long time, so one of the solutions was to find a daycare for dogs. I found a beautiful one, where there was field and land where he could play with more dogs and even a horse. It only took one day to realize that the other dogs were bullying him, so Galo spent time with the horse. It seemed very funny to me that he had made friends with a horse. Because he was so big, I thought maybe he saw himself closer to the horse than the other dogs, but it wasn't long before we discovered why he liked being with the horse so much. One day, when I went to pick him up, he was next to his horse friend, he saw me and, as always, he came running towards me, to greet me with his happy face, and I also happily waited for him with open arms, but as he got closer, I realized that his nose was all brown. At first, I thought it was dirt that he had been digging, digging a hole, but as soon as he got closer, I had no doubts thanks to the smell. Yes, Galo liked being with the horse so much because he liked to eat something that came from inside the horse... I remember that journey home as one of the worst in my life. The smell was unbearable; every time Galo gasped, you couldn't breathe in the car, despite having all the windows down and the air conditioning. It was the first time I had brushed a dog's teeth.

On the beach

My boy was also very fearful, to such an extent that he only needed a strong wind to not want to leave the house. If we were walking and he saw something strange on the street, for example, a construction container or a small mountain of gravel, he no longer wanted to walk in that direction and we had to turn around to find another alternative route... and we continued this way until Minnie, his sister, entered our lives.

I believe that when you share your life with an animal you experience some unforgettable moments. I´ve been very happy with my boys; I am convinced that much more than I would have been without them.

Sometime later, we picked up from the street a kitten that also ended up being part of our family. We lived together happily for a long time. Galo kept drooling, breaking up and enjoying life as only he knew how to do. However, one fine day, we went to visit the vet to treat a wound that had come out on his leg and, unfortunately, the wound was not such, but cancer. It was removed and he was treated with chemotherapy. Thanks to this he was able to live two and a half more years, with quality of life, being happy and up to his old tricks.

Galo did not change over time, he did not mature; as we say, he had Peter Pan syndrome. I remember one day, almost at the end of his life, when I got home with my husband (yes, Galo accompanied me from the stage of sharing a flat until I got married and formed my family) and opened the door, our first thought was that thieves had entered to rob us, until we realized that everything in between, on the floor, on the walls, on the sofa, everywhere, was food that we had in our fridge. I had never thought that a dog would be able to eat everything Galo ate, including a dozen uncooked eggs, in the shell and all, but hey, on the other hand, I had never thought that a dog could learn to open a refrigerator.

In the end, Galo was lucky, he left us in just a week. The cancer got worse and, although we tried different treatments to see if he would overcome it, his kidney no longer responded and there was nothing to do. I remember those sleepless days on the couch, my efforts for fim to get ahead, to keep hope. Those were days of trying to negotiate and beg fate to let me have him a little longer, but life simply passes by, it does not ask for permission or give in to blackmail.

I spoke with his veterinarian, Pedro, because I did not want to say goodbye to him on the floor of a veterinary office and he came home to euthanize him. When the doorbell rang, I was in shock. All I remember is that I didn't want to open the door, I didn't want to, but my legs moved by themselves, they carried me to the door and I opened it. I didn't want to do it, but it was what had to be done. I owed it to him, to me and to our love. Sometimes we have to do very difficult things for the ones we love. That is LOVE, in capital letters.

Galo went quietly, at home, on his bed and surrounded by his toys and carrot, with his mom lying on the floor, hugging him.

"It seemed to me that you were immortal, you have done so many pranks, you have digested such unthinkable things, that I believed that inside you were not flesh and blood, but a kind of terminator type machine".

The time has come to say goodbye, I caress him everywhere, I want my fingers and my memory to never forget where he had his spots and the shape of his pads. Tears in my eyes and kissing him everywhere, the little snout, that always fresh snout, the paws, the ears, the only thing

I could say to him was: "You have been the worst dog in the world, but the best one to teach me to love. Thank you for being my partner, I love you with all my heart. Wait for me in the rainbow".

Along with him, not only my dog left, a part of my life left too, the mischief, the laughter, the drool, the giant hugs, my single days. I didn't just cry for him, but for the end of a time in my life that I didn't want to end. I cried for everything we had lived through, but also for everything that would no longer be, for everything that we would no longer live together. Sometime later, when the pain subsided, I understood that life is that, stages, and the important thing is to learn from each one. I learned the meaning of unconditional love: I didn't need my dog to be the best dog in order to love him with all my heart.

"We are all the pieces of what we remember.
We have within us the hopes and fears of those
who love us. As long as there is love and memory,
there is no real loss".
(Cassandra Clare)

Our last photo

2. The time has come. Goodbye or see you soon?

O ne day, that dreaded moment simply arrives, that moment in which none of the people who have a four-legged friend want to think about, and it comes, you're ready or not.

Like everything written in this book, it´s very difficult to generalize; perhaps your partner had been ill for a long time; perhaps it was the result of old age or, on the contrary, he may have gone more unexpectedly, such as an accident or a rapid illness when he was still young; he may have left naturally or he had to be euthanized. These circumstances will mark, either to facilitate or to hinder the grieving process.

Sudden deaths are more difficult to assimilate, due to a lack of preparation. If to this is added a violent death, such as an accident or the attack of another animal, the feeling of stupefaction and pain is maximum. If we are not present, the incognito of the circumstances is sometimes worse than the knowledge of what happened and it generates an inherent sense of guilt. A prolonged illness that ends unfortunately in death is easier to digest, since many times the grieving process can begin while our partner is still alive, but in the knowledge that he will not recover, it is also incredibly hard to watch your little one suffering, unable to ease his pain. This creates distress and weakens the family. Many illnesses even seem to resolve and then get worse, and in the end, care can be stressful and exhausting. Quiet deaths after reaching old age, such as those that occur during sleep, give hope of an easy process, without suffering for our friend and they are, perhaps, the easiest to assimilate, because we find something to hold on to; our friend has left without suffering. Be that as it may, at that moment the world falls apart. You feel a crack in your heart that is opening its way and deepening, even physical pain and sadness very difficult to cope with, you cannot imagine your life without him, but you know that the time has come to the farewell.

In his last breath, there is little that I can tell you to ease your pain, only humbly ask you to try to facilitate the dying process within your possibilities; try to be by his side if possible; please, never leave them alone if they are going to be euthanized, they love you and need you, make this last gesture of unconditional love, to give back a little of as much as your furry has given you; you must transmit love, tranquility and one of the most powerful feelings in the world, gratitude. Try to create a peaceful and serene environment, and say goodbye by thanking him, gratitude for so much sharing, gratitude for having coincided in this life; you can give them internally or in a very low and calm voice: "See you soon. I love you. Until we meet again".

If you haven't been able to be with him in his last moments, don't worry, I assure you that he has been with you; when consciousness is clouded, that will have been its last image: you.

In these first moments, depending on the circumstances and the personality of each one, a state of shock can occur (see in the chapter dedicated to the stages of mourning). If this happens to us, it seems that we are in a cloud, that nothing that happens is real. We react this way because our brain becomes blocked in a situation that is difficult for us to assume. The state of shock can last minutes, hours or days, and although at first it may seem that it´s not doing any good to the person suffering from it, the truth is that it´s helping her to assimilate little by little that painful reality. It´s known that the brain quickly refuses to accept. In this phase, denial or disbelief usually occurs at the death of our animal. We cannot believe that our friend is gone, that we will never see him again, that he won´t be at home waiting, that we won´t enjoy our time together.

I personally am a person inclined to suffering a state of shock at the death of my furry. When my best childhood friend, Kira, passed away, I hugged her and hugged that body that I had loved so much and tried to remember all our moments together; after a few minutes (from my perception) they told me they had come to pick her up. The "minutes" I had been holding her had actually been 6 hours. Many years later, I have had to perform the hardest and most unconditional act of love that exists: euthanize my two children, Galo and Minnie. I suppose it´s a test that life puts in front of you, to see to what extent you are capable of loving another being, even above yourself. You know that letting go will be incredibly painful for you, but staying will be incredibly painful for them. When I had to euthanize Minnie, it all happened like an unconnected and incoherent dream, mixing conscious moments with others that are blurred in my mind. I was not able to speak, the tears did not allow me to see her little face resting completely on my hands. When her little nose stopped breathing in, a groan came from within me. How painful it is when a piece of your soul is ripped off!

The very purpose of this book is none other than to alleviate and help overcome such a sad fact as losing our furry companion. I know that it´s a very ambitious goal, since at this moment there will be nothing that can minimally ease the sadness and the pain you feel for this loss; the only thing I can tell you is that time is your friend and it´s in your favor. Although at first it may seem impossible that sorrow will diminish, I assure you that it will, to such an extent that one day you will be able to look back and remember your friend not with tears in your eyes but with a smile in your heart. And although at this moment, surely, the question that comes to mind is why? Why has he had to leave now? Why do animals live so little? Why did it have to happen to him? I ask you to try to change that "why?" for a "thank you". "Thank you" because I have had the opportunity to meet you, thank you for so many shared moments, thank you for having made this family so happy, thank you for having been our partner.

Sometimes, what our perception receives as a "goodbye", is actually just a "see you soon". I firmly believe that we come into this life to learn lessons; some people learn them very quickly, while others stumble over the same stone countless times. I am sure that if you look around you, you will also perceive it. Those things that we need to grow happen to us; many times, they are painful and it´s very difficult to understand it when they happen to ourselves, but if you look at the people around you, perhaps, you can discover them more easily. I am convinced that animals have fewer lessons to learn than we do, without egos, without greed, without evil, living in the present, loving unconditionally... It´s clear to me that it takes us a lifetime to reach that level. If we reach it. No wonder they need to be less time here on Earth, because they already know much more about life than us.

A DOG HAS DIED

My dog has died.
I buried him in the garden
next to a rusted old machine.

Some day I'll join him right there,
but now he's gone with his shaggy coat,
his bad manners and his cold nose,
and I, the materialist, who never believed
in any promised heaven in the sky
for any human being,
I believe in a heaven I'll never enter.
Yes, I believe in a heaven for all dogdom
where my dog waits for my arrival
waving his fan-like tail in friendship.

Ai, I'll not speak of sadness here on earth,
of having lost a companion

who was never servile.
His friendship for me, like that of a porcupine
withholding its authority,
was the friendship of a star, aloof,
with no more intimacy than was called for,
with no exaggerations:
he never climbed all over my clothes
filling me full of his hair or his mange,
he never rubbed up against my knee
like other dogs obsessed with sex.

No, my dog used to gaze at me,
paying me the attention I need,
the attention required
to make a vain person like me understand
that, being a dog, he was wasting time,
but, with those eyes so much purer than mine,
he'd keep on gazing at me
with a look that reserved for me alone
all his sweet and shaggy life,
always near me, never troubling me,
and asking nothing.

Ai, how many times have I envied his tail
as we walked together on the shores of the sea

in the lonely winter of Isla Negra
where the wintering birds filled the sky
and my hairy dog was jumping about
full of the voltage of the sea's movement:
my wandering dog, sniffing away
with his golden tail held high,
face to face with the ocean's spray.

Joyful, joyful, joyful,
as only dogs know how to be happy
with only the autonomy
of their shameless spirit.

There are no good-byes for my dog who has died,
and we don't now and never did lie to each other.

So now he's gone and I buried him,
and that's all there is to it.

(Pablo Neruda)

3. Death: from living among us to living in us

I'm going to ask a very direct question: "Do you think about your death?"

I suppose that for many people it´s not a very pleasant question, but I will be honest, whether you are religious or atheist, you should not avoid thinking about it. The inevitability of death, both yours and those around you, is your best asset to live. We are sure only of one thing in this life and that is that we are going to die.

They teach us many things in our student years, but unfortunately, they do not teach us some of the most important things, such as facing death. From a young age, we spend a lot of time learning things like math, language or even drawing, but no one teaches us to cope with death, grief or separation from those we love the most. None of us have received training to understand the process we have to go through when saying goodbye to someone we love, what emotions we are going to feel, what functions they perform, how to manage it and what things can help us to cope... This is very simple; we have not received emotional education.

Surely, if we lived under the certainty of death, we would make many decisions in a completely different way than we do now. Would you worry about trivial things if you assumed that sooner or later you were going to die? Would you get angry with certain people many times over trifles knowing that your time with that being is limited? Would you try to fulfill your dreams knowing that your life is ephemeral? We are here for a short time and we do not have to live our life to please other people or get a reputation, but we have to live our life, simply, to enjoy it and enjoy all that surrounds us. Let me remind you of something we know, but often forget; when the time comes, both yours and your loved ones, what we are going to take with us will not be the job we have had or the model of the car we have bought or the iPhone or brand clothing; at that moment, what will remain in our hearts will be the moments that we have shared in company; the walks, the beach days, the trips, the meals all together... that is what we are going to take with us, so your energies should be directed towards that.

Does your furry friend prefer that you buy him a bone from the best brand possible and leave him at home chewing it or spend an afternoon of games together in the park? Create the life that you want, create the moments you want to take with you, because that is the only thing you will have left. THAT IS THE REAL IMPORTANT THING.

Death is painful because we perceive it as a break. What united us to that beloved animal has been broken, we are separated in time and space. This causes us great pain because we want our partner with us, we want to see him once more, to be able to hug him and enjoy him, but... what if I told you that death is not a break but simply a change. We oppose death, we fight against it, we cry and we are filled with rage and helplessness, we walk along the path of our mourning to finally accept that that so loved being is no more. Here, many people will have their own idea of death, based on religion or atheism; for some, there will be heaven; for others reincarnation, and for some, simply nothingness. Our beliefs also influence the moment of mourning for our furry. Obviously, having a positive and spiritual opinion of death is one more comfort, which can slightly illuminate our path. There is no one who can confirm to us that death leads to the complete destruction of being. My advice is that you choose the most positive, hopeful and beautiful scenario that you can, instead of surrendering to the blackest and depressing panorama possible; nothing is proven, nobody knows what is there; so why stick with the worst? (see chapter "The Legend of the Rainbow Bridge").

It's something difficult to assimilate, but believe me when I tell you that there is no separation, because that union that we have experienced with our loved ones is unbreakable. The bonds that united us to our furry were not only on a physical level, but on a much higher plane and there will come a time when you will see that you have been given a great gift: share a priceless time with your partner and that is all you need, keep it inside yourself forever, while you live there will no longer be separation. I'm certainly not here to tell you where your friend is or what you should believe, but let me tell you something: he has not left and will never leave, even if you feel it as a separation, the truth is that a part of your partner will always be with you and this is not something spiritual or unrealistic, its a fact. They go from living among us to living WITHIN us. Each person or animal that crosses our lives, with whom we share a home, moments and time, change us, it works as a power in us; he teaches us things and although it seems that he is leaving, because he is no longer with us physically, the truth is that the time we have shared has changed us, it has made us different and a part of them has entered into us; so, we will always be united by this. Surely, we would not be the same people if we had not met a particular being, if we had not been born into a certain family; we would not have lived the same life, we would not have learned the same lessons, so we can think that what we are is a mixture or is seasoned by all the people and animals who have bonded with us and, even if that bond is broken somehow, a part of them will always be immersed within our personality and our heart; that bond can be broken physically, but it will not break psychically and emotionally. Love does not end because of the presence or absence of the loved one, love remains beyond that and it is precisely that love that will continue to hold us together, each time we remember it, each time our shared stories come to mind and we focus on the happy moments, we will fill ourselves with all the good of that being that we love and that will live forever in us.

For me personally, each animal that I have loved has taught me something, he has made me learn, he has made me better. From the sweetness of Kira, my first partner with whom I shared a bed from 9 to 24 years old; through Gala and King, who taught me innocence; following Galo, who taught me patience and unconditional love since, as you know, he was the worst dog in the world, and yet I loved him every day of his life and I will love him every day of mine, and ending with Minnie, who taught me the power of love because, truly, love can change everything. When I adopted her, I made her ending our beginning and she made me discover how grateful it can be to help others.

Each one, like each one of those who are still with me, has left a little piece of them in my heart, they teach me and mold me and I am what I am also thanks to them.

"It came to me that every time I lose a dog they take a piece of my heart with them. And every new dog who comes into my life, gifts me with a piece of their heart. If I live long enough, all the components of my heart will be dog, and I will become as generous and loving as they are".
(Unknown)

"We learnt a lot about the loss thanks
to the dying. Those who have been technically
dead and been brought back to life they convey
some clear and simple lessons. First, they
claim to have lost their fear of death. Second,
they say they now know that death is only
discarding from physical body, much like
taking off a set of clothes that are no longer
needed. Third, they remember having a deep
sense of integrity in death, have felt connected to
everything and everyone, without any
sense of loss. Finally, we know that they were
never alone, someone was with them".
(Elisabeth Kübler-Ross, "Life Lessons")

4. The mourning

Although the words grief and mourning may seem to mean the same thing, they do not. They correspond to different processes related to the loss of a loved one.

Grief is the moderately formalized expression of responding to the death of someone close to us; I mean the external display of feelings of sorrow, mourning and respect for the deceased and his family. This includes wakes, funerals and dark colored clothing, among others, and it´s different in every society.

Grieving can also be giving a few days to yourself, to assimilate what has happened, it´s like a stand-by. If you need it, please do it. In fact, it is highly recommended; it has been shown that after a loss, people who choose to return to their work, their normal life, attend parties, put on a good face to not add more distress to the family... can extend much longer the period of mourning that follows grieving.

Currently, in many parts of Spain, we already have the possibility of vigil and carrying out a farewell rite of our friends. We can incinerate them and recover their ashes to keep them with us and there are even cemeteries for pets where we can bury them under their own tombstone, to go to remember them. We also have the possibility of acquiring biodegradable urns with seeds that will become trees, which will make us remember our loved one.

Funeral jewelry or also known as ash storage pendants, allow us to treasure the ashes of our animals inside. They are pieces that you can carry with you at all times, like any traditional jewel. They come in different shapes and sizes and appear to be normal ornaments so no one will know they are funeral homes if you don't want to share that. These concepts have gained importance recently, as they have multiple benefits. They provide peace, tranquility and serenity, by being able to feel a part of our colleagues close to us, whether in an urn with their photo, a pendant or a tree. This proliferation of mortuary accessories is due to the fact that more and more people refuse to say goodbye to their friend on a cold table in a vet's office.

In this particular moment, the beliefs of each one and their level of spirituality will also come into play. What is clear is that any ritual to say goodbye to our furry, be it watching over them, writing a letter, crying the whole family together for a few hours or performing a symbolic act, it helps us to accept the reality of the situation, to say goodbye and to remove any feelings that became embedded inside: I should have realized before that he was sick, I wish I hadn't left open the door through which he escaped, I should have done more things with him... dragging a feeling of guilt that, many times, can be generated by the loss.

These rituals are an act of love towards our companions, but also towards ourselves. There will be people who will feel more comfortable doing them alone; however, if it's a united family facing pain, it's much better to do it all together. You can organize a ritual, even a few days or weeks after death, when it is a little calmer, somewhere that your little one will especially like, somewhere prepared for this in your area or at home. The idea is to write a farewell letter or improvise a few words. Always try to be positive, remembering the good times more and focusing on happy aspects rather than sad ones, each one to the best of his ability. Children (see chapter "Grief in children") can draw a picture or dictate to an adult what they want to say. Once in the chosen place, the letters, poems, songs, drawings... will be read and then burned in a safe place or they will be broken or whatever each one decides, although I do not suggest saving them, but letting them go.

In this act, it's important not to repress ourselves; if you have to cry, cry; if you feel like being sad or cranky, do it. The important thing is to open ourselves to what we feel, to bring out everything that is inside, without judging our own feelings or those of others. Untold feelings die within us. Shared pain hurts less.

In the first moments of the loss of their friend, some people may find themselves unable to perform any ritual or ceremony; however, they can celebrate it later; for example, if we want to spread the ashes (see where it can be done in each region) or you can carry out a small act on a certain date such as the anniversary of death or birthday, giving the possibility to family and friends who want to participate and respect those who do not feel that way. Establish a specific time for the ritual, with a developed structure of beginning, body and closing. The best thing is to use this time to remember the good moments enjoyed with our friend, to be grateful for the time with him and all that we have learned and lived; express what he has meant and continues to mean to us and remember his pranks, adding a touch of humor if that is what we feel; also removing those little thorns that could have embedded in our hearts, like some feeling of anger or even asking for forgiveness if we consider it that way. Always remember that what hurts us the most are precisely the thoughts that we do not express, so this is a good opportunity to empty the backpack that we often carry on our shoulders.

Some people may judge this as silly or unnecessary; however, I don't know of anyone who has done it and has regretted it. Sometimes the simplest ritual, such as seeing some photos and videos with the whole family together and each one saying a few words, can be a very beautiful and emotional experience that will be worth living.

These celebrations mark the end of a stage and are an excellent opportunity to be together, united and share as a family, remembering all the good times we have spent with our friend and giving thanks for having been able to share with him.

Now you only need time and that time -that we must allow ourselves to heal our wounds internally- is mourning.

The little corner of the San Juan Park, Alicante. Each tape is in honor of a furry that left; there we do our farewell ritual. If there is not something like this in your city, surely you can propose it yourself. In the poster can be read:

"A little corner where to remember those little four-legged angels that are gone and that we loved so much and to rememeber how much they gave us. If you also have a furry friend that you want to honor, put on a ribbon".

"That the dog only lives 15 years is a scam of love".
(Unknown)

"Do not cry because it's over, smile because
it happened".
(Gabriel Garcia Marquez)

5. The grief: living the absence

Losing your friend means a breakup more or less un-expected, compared to what your life has been up to that point. From now on, everything changes and we need some time to adapt. Grief is a hard, sad and difficult time, where emotions and feelings labelled as "not pleas-ant" intermingle, which can vary from confusion, guilt, anger, longing, hopelessness, sadness... although person-ally I think that the "not pleasant" thing would be never to feel them, because it would mean that we don't know how to love, that we are people with little capacity to feel. How sad that must be!

Don't worry about having all this confusion inside you, grief is nothing more than a natural response to a fact that is also natural and inextricably linked to life. It's a period that, although at first we do not understand, it's going to bring us a lot of personal growth, many teachings about the value of time, the preciousness of shared moments and it will bring us closer to our interior and ourselves, things that would otherwise go unnoticed, given the non-stop rhythm of life that currently governs our time. Stop, talk to yourself, name the feelings that flow inside you, get used to looking at your thoughts from the outside, without judging yourself, as if you were a simple spectator, illuminate what is happening inside you and learn to know yourself.

Do not be ashamed to suffer for your furry companion, be honest with yourself and your feelings, because you have loved and cared for him as a member of the family and, consequently, it´s logical and normal that his death affects you. Honestly, I find much more shameful the fact that some people, after having an animal by their side for years, hardly feel anything for their departure; there are even those who abandon their animals during old age. That is what should be a source of shame, not having the capacity to love. Not having empathy or compassion shows that there is a cold and dry heart within these people. You, on the other hand, prove to be someone with a soul, capable of opening your heart and feeling in all its fullness. What difference does it make if your neighbor, your brother-in-law or your co-worker doesn't understand? There is only one person to whom you owe something, to whom you owe sincerity and coherence, and that person is the one who looks at you every morning from the mirror.

The emotional pain we feel when we have lost an important being in our lives is a normal process; some people are surprised because they suffer more from the death of their pet than the death of a relative; we should not worry or feel bad about it, everything has an explanation. When we lose a loved one, we must adjust to life without him; this is one of the most painful processes that we must overcome, it´s much harder to change our daily routines (the walks, the time to get home, the space left in the living room where his bed used to be...) than for example, adjusting to the routine when a distant uncle that we saw twice a year passes away. In the latter case, our day to day does not change, we will miss him in family gatherings and we will remember our conversations and his humor, but we will not have the constant weight of his absence, since our life will remain practically the same in its habits. Not surprisingly, the factors that most often influence grief are the sociocultural environment, the intensity of the union and the proximity of coexistence. So don't worry, you are not a weirdo or a bad person. If you spent many hours with your furry, you slept together, you enjoyed games or daily walks, it´s completely normal that your grief for him is more difficult to work out than the one for some people from your more distant environment. I know that saying this is politically incorrect in our society and that it´s quite a taboo subject, but I think it´s time to open this door and be able to express the love we feel for our animals, without feeling fear that the typical criticisms will appear: " What's wrong, you love animals more than people?" Man, it depends on what animal and what person.

When our partner leaves, many times we find ourselves without a motor, because he was a motivation for some aspects of our life; then the grief just becomes one more grief; I not only mourn his absence, but those parts of me that will no longer be. I also cry for the past, because it´s a piece of my life that has been taken from me; all that we have lived together, all our common projections has remained incomplete. I cry for my friend, but I also cry for myself. Personally, I really enjoy hiking in the mountains and I was always accompanied by my furry Minnie, the two of us always walking along the trails, enjoying the views, resting in beautiful places and sharing that connection with nature... When she left, I was unable for some time to return to "our mountain", I felt strange, out of place and more alone than ever. My own unique presence suffocated me, in a constant memory of her absence. The feeling of helplessness is not only because my girl has left, but because our days of excursions have gone, also enjoying those walks and those views, because for me an important part was sharing it with her; even my ability to enjoy is totally diminished, since I lack the enjoyment of that little girl that I always had by my side and that, without realizing it, enhanced the way I enjoyed things. I also remember the pain of assuming that no other being would ever look at me like her, my reflection in her eyes looking at me with the love, devotion and tenderness of someone who knew she had had a second chance thanks to me. I cried a lot for that part of me that will no longer be and for what it made me feel. This is called the mourning for the broken mirror, it´s the mourning for that facet of our personality that our partner was able to bring out of us and that without him it´s no longer there. An example would be that of a man of mature age, businessman, quite serious and imposing, who disconsolately commented to me that he had been that strict person that everyone saw for years, except when he played with his dog; then he was a teenager again and they had fun together like children. Now that his dog was gone, that side was gone with him and he was left with only his part of a serious, solemn businessman. Overcoming grief is also being ourselves again, filling that void within us.

We have to go through the pain, an almost physical slap in the center of our being, which is usually caused by anything that reminds us of our missing friend: his bed, the strap, the toy that he liked so much... it even seems necessary that we get rid of those objects that cause us so much pain but, on the other hand, we do not want to let go of the memories, we do not want to clean our pain, putting aside those things that, although they cause us suffering, seem to be the bond we now have with our friend. You don't need to get rid of everything, nor is it necessary to keep everything; remember that pushing away is not the same as overcoming. If you try to get rid of everything so that you wouldn´t think about your grief, you are not overcoming it, but only hiding and it will remain pending within you; besides, after a while, you will surely regret not having kept even a small memory of him. If you want to get rid of everything and you don't need to have anything physical from your partner because you have him in your heart, that´s fine with me. Remember to donate all the things of your furry to the closest Animal Protection Association or animal shelter, because even in his last moments, he will be doing an act of love for his equals. Nor should you keep all his things as if he were still here, since it is a way of denying the reality of death, it is an avoidance maneuver; in these cases, it´s best to set times to gradually separate yourself from his things and commit to those "deadlines".

Grief affects us in different ways: physical, emotional, intellectual, behavioral and spiritual. In the period of mourning, the reaction is as personal as people are suffering it; like everything else, in this book it´s practically impossible to generalize, but we are going to try to name below the most common and completely natural reactions that usually occur. If you suffer them, remember to be calm, because it´s something normal.

The physical responses to grief can be: exhaustion, insomnia, shortness of breath, pain in the jaw and/or bruxism, loss of appetite, anxiety and pain in different parts of the body (abdomen, head, back, neck or joints).

The emotional responses are usually: sadness, anger, rage, despair, fear, guilt, irritability, restlessness, vulnerability, confusion and longing.

The mental or intellectual responses can be: disbelief, inability to concentrate, loss of intellectual capacity, going blank, obsessive thoughts about what happened, dreaming of our friend, feeling his presence, visiting places of memory or avoiding them and treasuring souvenir things.

Behavioral responses such as apathy, reluctance or hyperactivity, working hard and keeping busy, inability to be alone, or isolation and forgetting things.

Some people, during the days or weeks after death, will not feel like doing practically any activity, while others will tend to be busier than usual, since inactivity can accentuate their pain. It´s very important not to judge any of the above behaviors; one person did not love his partner more than other person, we have to understand that not all of us manage pain in the same way. Although this attitude often seems like indifference, it´s fundamental for those who are going through this stage not to make comparisons, each person will know internally what his body asks of him and will have his times.

The most important thing when we elaborate grief is to give ourselves freedom to feel, recognize our own needs and respect them and be able to share our emotions without being ashamed, in a safe environment, where we feel understood and without being judged, without feeling strange for having these feelings towards an animal, because of course, for many people it was "just a dog / cat / rabbit / parrot". Animals love us without conditions, they take care of us, they make us happy, they never disappoint or deceive us, they are pure innocence, without any evil, without arguments or absurd egos, without impositions... isn't it completely normal that we correspond by giving them a place in our hearts? It´s incredible how two different species can love each other like this... I think that´s just wonderful!

A study recently revealed that we bond with our animals in the same way that we bond with other people. The same hormones and chemicals are released into our brains, making us feel loved, connected, and on the same page, regardless of species. The only difference between mourning for your furry and another for a relative is the understanding that you will receive from your environment. A patient told me that what had hurt the most was not receiving condolences or a word of comfort from people very close to her, people who would have called her because of the death of a distant uncle, but who did not consider it important when her furry died.

It can be a common thing not to feel supported by your environment during the mourning for your partner and it is possible that many people are not up to the circumstances and not up to your feelings for the loss of your friend; some because they won't know what to say to you, others because they won't even understand what you're going through, especially people who don't have animals or who don't treat them like a member of their family. Feeling that lack of understanding will cause you another suffering, it´s what is called accumulated or secondary loss. That will sum up to your grief the added pain of seeing how certain people behave indifferently, say inappropriate things or even, they make fun of your feelings. It´s true that all this does a lot of damage, but unfortunately there are many people who do not have the gift of empathy, nobody has taught them to accompany, to listen; they do not know what a privilege it is to love an animal with all their heart, poor people! Be patient even with those who have hurt you the most, because as we say here *"don't ask for pears from the elm tree"*. We must ask each one to the extent each can give, not more. Lean on those people who you feel can understand you; if not, you can seek help from me or from any other professional or join our grieving group or some other.

Let me ask you a question: "Which grief is better? Is it a good grief of the person´s who removes all the photos of his partner, who throws everything in the trash, not wanting anyone to mention his name or not wanting to talk about him, who runs away from all the places they went together and no one saw him cry or it will be better the grief of the person who treasures one of his photos as if it were a gift, who has donated the bed, the feeder and the food he had left, but nevertheless keeps his favorite toy, each time he talks about him tears fill his eyes, but he can't help remember him very often?".

I don't think I need to tell you that the second mourning is not only better, but it is even healthy and restorative. You have to learn to live your suffering, because without it you will not grow, you will not be reborn. How can you truly enjoy happiness without experiencing sadness? Many people, however, are afraid of sadness and may try to suppress the pain without doing this work of mourning, which could lead to hiding everything inside. We would alleviate the outer suffering a little, but the wound that is still closed will continue to fester inside us, never resolved, never learning to face the difficult moments of our life, without tools to face them and reappearing in future events.

Emotional crises (loss, divorce, illness) are a great opportunity for us; they will never cease to exist, since it´s not something we can control, so we have two options: learn from them and get out reinforced or go through these situations without pain or glory, rejecting any learning, so that when the next one occurs, we will be left again as they usually say "like a dazzled rabbit".

I want you to write down this word somewhere that you see often, like in the bathroom mirror, inside the closet door, the screen of your mobile or tablet or your bedside table: RESILIENCE. This word comes from the Latin *resilio* and means "to bounce, jump and jump again, restart"; refers to the ability of steel to return to its original shape, despite the blows it may receive. In psychology, it´s used to describe the ability to live unfavourable experiences and emerge strengthened from them. It is personal growth after adversity, where a person discovers new capacities that were previously unknown, feeling more secure to face other experiences. This leads to a life change, a new philosophy of life that reinforces us and brings light to times of darkness.

Some aspects that can make the grief more traumatic are the following: if you think that death could have been avoided, if you think that your partner has suffered, if you lack details and information about how the death was that make it impossible to understand it, the death was traumatic and you witnessed it, if your partner died after an illness where many moments of hope and despair alternated and if the way you received the news was inappropriate.

Not knowing how your partner's last moments have been is something that can torture you; the suffering we see is easier to bear, yet the imagined, that of which we know nothing about, grows in the darkness of our imagination. The worst suffering is the one we cannot measure; you have not been able to be present, therefore, you do not know what happened. It could be a traffic accident, a domestic accident, a fight with another animal, a fire... in your brain that moment has no end, you go round and round, imagining what will have happened. For you that moment is repeated over and over again. Let me tell you something, physical suffering always ends, it has a beginning and an end, remember that even if your friend suffered, it is impossible for you to know to what degree; even, surely it is much less than what you are imagining. Remember that the body goes into a state of shock in an accident and stops feeling pain; besides, that moment has already passed, it had its end; it´s your brain that relives it over and over again.

"We've done what we could," says the vet.

That thought seems to ease a part of the pain, that of thinking that something else could have been done, but especially if the death was accidental, sudden or due to a short illness, people in mourning often explain that in their head they can be repeated thoughts obsessively, the famous "and if...": "and if he had tried another vet, we would have realized before he was sick, that car would not have passed..." (these thoughts are also related to guilt, a normal feeling in the elaboration of the grief). Making a good grief is accepting that we are not omnipotent, that we cannot control everything, that life is fragile. Like for any human being, it´s difficult to accept the unpredictability of life, when we live in a society in which we always have everything under control. We never allow ourselves to improvise, our life is completely organized, but I am sorry to tell you that, despite everything, unforeseen things continue to happen, we continue to be subjected to chance and the fragility of life. We must be humble and aware that we did what we could at that time, under those circumstances and with the information we had. I do not have control over life, life simply is, and I assume and accept it, I flow with the current of the river, instead of fighting against it, because I will only end up exhausted and full of wounds.

We can say that we have completed a grief process when we are able to remember our companions without feeling such intense pain, when we have stopped living focusing only on the past and we keep a fond memory of the time we have enjoyed with our furry. Each person has their own rhythm that we could place between 3 months to 12 or even 24 months. After this time, we would have a complicated duel and we should seek psychological help.

"To elaborate grief is to transform pain into love".
(Alba Payàs P.)

6. The stages of grief

S ince 1969, in this field of psychology, the theory of the five phases of grief is dominant, developed by the Swiss-American psychiatrist Elisabeth Kübler-Ross, who was and is, even today, one of the world's leading experts in death, dying people and palliative care, for which she received 23 honorary doctorates. This woman endowed the terminally ill and their families with integrity, when this topic was still a taboo in society and among doctors themselves, to the point that there was no protocol to follow in hospitals.

In her book "On Death and Dying," she presented this general model of five stages of grief, which explain how people feel at different times and how they tend to act. In that and twelve other works, she laid the foundations for modern palliative care, the purpose of which is for the patient to face death with serenity and even joy.

1. Denial stage

This denial can initially soften the impact of the death of a loved one and postpone some of the pain, but this stage cannot be indefinite because at some point it will collide with reality (*I do not believe that it is gone, this cannot be...*). In these first moments, the state of shock occurs; the most characteristic thing is that the person who suffers feels detached from reality, without temporal perception; he is puzzled and confused and works automatically; some people behave as if nothing had happened, empty of feelings, while others are practically paralyzed. The state of shock and denial are fundamental in grief and a precious help, since they are protective states that gradually let the pain pass to us, instead of having to face it suddenly.

2. Stage of anger

When the reality of death can no longer be avoided and the state of shock disappears, we begin to walk the path of anger. This stage usually manifests itself with the expulsion of repressed feelings in the first stage of grief and it´s usually expressed by an explosion of emotions and feelings; feelings of anger, resentment and even aggressiveness are characteristic, as well as the search for those responsible or guilty. Anger appears before the frustration that death is irreversible, that there is no possible solution and that anger can be projected towards the environment, including family members or other close people (*it's the vet's fault, dad never loved our furry, I won't love any other animal...*). Anger can also splatter, even, the neighbor who has nothing to do with what happened (*"why has this happened to my cat with how well cared he was and not to my neighbor's who treats his in any way?"*). One of the most common and most difficult anger to overcome is the one we project onto ourselves. Let us remember that underneath this anger and this whirlwind of angry feelings lies great pain. Anger is a source of energy that keeps us from sinking. At this stage, it´s very important that people can express all their anger and rage without being judged; sometimes resentment can cause them to say horrible things, but it´s necessary in order to move on and through this phase. Let us remember that it´s pain that speaks. Anger is what we call a cover emotion: as long as we feel it, the pain will be disguised in the background. If anger is not expressed, it ends up turning into a feeling of bitterness and resentment that can be very destructive for the person suffering from it.

3. Negotiation stage

In this phase, people fantasize that the fact of death can be reversed or changed. The negotiation stage can occur before the loss, in the event that the companion animal has suffered a terminal illness, or after death, to try to negotiate the pain caused by this distance. It is common to offer promises and changes in us, in order to have our friend back or, on the contrary, ask ourselves: "what if ...?" or think of strategies that would have prevented the final result, such as: "What if I had done this or that?" (*if I had taken him to another vet, if I had been at home on the day of the accident...*). During this stage, we stop living in the present to move into the past and try to find a solution or some other deviation that leads us to another reality, a reality in which our friend is still here physically. In this phase, obsessive and repetitive thoughts about the events leading up to death may appear. It´s important to let the person express them, even if we see that he hurts himself with this attitude. Let us remember that everything we say we expel outside of ourselves; it´s much better to remove it than hide it inside us, so we will have to be patient and remember that these stages are temporary, just paths that we go through to reach the end of the grieving process. It is usually a short stage.

4. Stage of depression

In this stage it´s when death begins to be accepted as an irreparable fact and it´s marked by crying. We live again in the present, so deep sadness and the feeling of emptiness are characteristic of this phase, whose name does not refer to a clinical depression, such as a mental health problem, but to a set of emotions linked to sadness, natural to the loss of a loved one and, therefore, temporary. Some people may feel that they have no incentive to continue living in their day-to-day lives, without their dear friend and they may isolate themselves from their environment ("I don´t wanna *do nothing, why am I going to get out of bed...*"). This stage, although it´s usually one of the hardest and most extensive in time, it´s also the one that opens the way to acceptance. Remember the importance of accompaniment in these moments, since the person who suffers needs to let out all her pain. At the beginning of this period, advice or trying to be positive will not help, simply accompany with respect and listen, as the sufferer progresses, he will begin to listen and admit the words of others.

5. Acceptance stage

The end of the road. Once the loss is accepted, the grieving people learn to live with their emotional pain, in a world in which the loved one is no longer there. Over time, they regain their ability to experience joy and pleasure. It´s about accepting that the stones that we find in life are also part of the journey. It´s not easy to get here, but we have made it. We feel closer than ever to our partner and we continue our learning process, in this opportunity called life. You know that you are on the road to acceptance, when you no longer think so much about how the events of death occurred or because you are no longer looking for guilty parties, you can look at their photos and memories and, even if you still feel sadness inside, it´s not a stab of pain; you can talk about him and, although you get excited, it´s not an overreaction. You remember happy moments more than painful ones; you don't need to do so many exercises (see chapter "Coming out of the labyrinth") to feel good; you feel that everything was worth it and you are very grateful for the time shared.

According to experts, people do not necessarily go through all these stages or in that specific order, so grief can manifest itself in different ways and at different times for each person, jumping between these stages; even without suffering any of them or living just one stage two or more times, with different duration to overcome each one. Do not despair, remember that each step you are taking is a step already taken. The way in which we manage grief and emotions, learning to recognize them and knowing what they are for, makes it possible for us to experience personal growth during this process, to change our scale of values, to readjust the priorities in our life or perhaps it may even lead us to reconsider or change friendships.

We can know that we are facing a complicated grief when we settle on feelings such as anger, guilt or deep mourning, which prevents us from continuing to elaborate our grief process. We are not able to advance in any of the stages and we remain anchored to it. It could be defined as "the intensification of grief to the level in which the person is overwhelmed, resorts to maladaptive behaviors or remains endlessly in this state without advancing in the grief process towards its resolution" (Horowitz, 1980).

Generally, one of these four subtypes of complicated grief occurs:

- Chronic grief. After 12 or 24 months, the suffering continues practically as at the beginning. The bereaved still does not accept the pain, the anguish or the anxiety that he feels when remembering the loss. There is a retention in some of the stages, without the person being able to follow the path of mourning.

- Delayed or postponed grief. The person who apparently has better reacted to the loss (for this reason, reacting too well is not good) and who seemed to have accepted it in the best way, after a while experiences again a strong emotional charge, before some event that reopens the wound. The mourning is not over but hidden, so it resurfaces again.

- Exaggerated grief. The person feels overwhelmed with pain and tries to escape through certain avoidance behaviors, such as excessive consumption of alcohol or drugs, obsessively focusing on work, going out, or any behavior that allows them to cope with pain, which can lead to, ultimately, develop a psychopathological disorder, such as anxiety or depression problems. It may be that the person is aware that they are doing all this to avoid the pain that the loss implies, but they do not know how to deal with it.

- Masked grief. The person believes that they have overcome the grief, when they begin to present physical or psychological problems, such as psychopathological illnesses (anorexia, bulimia, anxiety...), but without realizing that these have to do with the loss that has not been overcome.

Faced with these types of complications, the intervention of a professional is necessary; he has to identify the tasks that have not been carried out and help the person to complete them.

Overcoming grief is something that is achieved progressively, not over night. Let us remember that they are paths that we must go through and sometimes they cross each other and make us feel lost, but as we walk through its streets, we go through stages: overcome the state of shock, accept the reality of loss, let go of all our anger, give way to our pain and live it fully, readjust our life without our partner, give him a new place in our minds and hearts.

Little by little, we begin to enjoy more the memories, we look at the past with love and longing, not with heartbroken grief. Although we can suffer some relapses on certain dates such as birthdays, Christmas or the anniversary of death, the rest of the time we are fine. Don't worry, a day will come when even those dates will be the cause of beautiful memories and not of suffering.

"Eventually we lose everything we have,
but what matters ultimately is never lost.
Our houses, cars, jobs and money, our youth and
even loved ones have only been borrowed.
Like everything else, we cannot always keep our
loved ones. But acceptance of this truth does
not have to make us sad. On the contrary, it may
provide the ability to better evaluate the myriad
of experiences and wonderful things we have for
as long as we stay here (on Earth)".
(Elisabeth Kübler-Ross, "Life Lessons")

7. Grief in a child

Nowadays, there is a taboo with death and loss in general. We push it aside and hide this kind of things and, for this lack of spontaneity, it´s impossible to know how to face them. If this happens in adults, in children it´s even worse. As parents, we are not prepared for these situations ourselves, so how are we going to inculcate in our children resources that we do not have?

In the past, the deceased were watched at home, the family itself washed and prepared them, and all this, under the look of the little ones. This gave rise to them being able to ask about death, to see it as something inherent in life, to normalize it. Currently, in Spain, there are funeral homes, where wakes are held far from the family nucleus, which has made it much easier for society to separate and exclude children from everything that has to do with death.

Often times, grieving for a pet will be the first experience children will have with the loss of a loved one. It´s much more advisable that you teach your children to face it with their own resources, from an early age, instead of waiting for another death to arrive, which will surely be more difficult. I am firmly convinced that one of the most important things you should teach your children (for me the most) is to respect life. Life is the most valuable thing for any living being; Bradley M. already said: *"Teaching a child not to step on a caterpillar is as valuable for the child as it is for the caterpillar."* Teaching your children how valuable a life is happens precisely by teaching them that life is fragile and irreplaceable.

Surely, the most common mistake that occurs with our children's domestic animals is not taking advantage of the opportunity and the great learning that is presented to us when the end of physical life arrives; instead of living it naturally and explaining this important information to our children, what we do is put a patch, cover it quickly and if it´s possible for the child not to find out about it, the better. In my years as a veterinary assistant, I have seen countless parents looking for the same hamster as their son had to give him "the change", the parakeet with the same colors, the identical minnow... or even worse, when his dog or cat dies, as it is impossible to replace him without the child noticing the difference, what we do is give him another one immediately after the loss, so that the child wouldn´t be sad not even for a day. Please, even if you have small children, I beg you not to teach that lesson to your children, not to overprotect them from something that is inherent in life and that, sooner or later, will come into their world. I fully understand that, very often, as parents, our reflex is to try to avoid suffering as much as possible for our children, but let me remind you that the best thing you can do for your children is to instill values in them. What value do you think you are teaching them, when you show them that one life can be replaced by another? When you don't let your son mourn his animal, because you immediately go to the store and buy him another, what do you think he is learning?

Do you think you can do the same when the one who is missing is your grandfather or grandmother?

The question is not as easy as just talking about it, but good communication. Do you remember everything we have seen about grief, expressing feelings, the need for understanding and so on? Well, that and some other variant, depending on the age, is what the children will need. And above all, empathy and respect, like any adult. Let's see an example:

You are 5 years old and your beloved hamster has just died.

1. Right away, your father buys the same one, he tells you that he has shrunk because he got sick. You don't know anything about the subject, you don't

learn anything and you don't generate resources because "nothing has happened".

2. When you wake up, you find your dead hamster, you yell out to Mom and Mom tells you that nothing is wrong, it´s just a hamster. If you are a boy, she will tell you that big and brave children do not cry; if you are a girl, if you cry you will become ugly. *It's just a hamster, don't make a tragedy of this nonsense.* You do not understand what is happening and you repress your feelings and emotions; you learn to keep everything inside and not express it.

3. You see your dead friend and, very worried, you call dad; you don't know what happens to your little animal. Dad tells you that nothing is wrong, that he is "just" dead and that it´s best to forget about him and do not talk about it again. He throws him in the trash and tells you that if you behave, he will buy you another tomorrow. You don't understand that life is precious, the other way around; the next day you have another hamster and it´s as if the first one never existed. You learn that living beings are substitutable like toys and that you can use them without giving them importance. Substitution is nothing more than an avoidance maneuver.

4. You return from school one day and your parents tell you that your hamster has gone on a trip, that he has escaped or that he has gone around the

world, in a space rocket. You don't understand why your friend has left...: *"Should I have taken more care of him? Is it my fault? Didn't he love me anymore?"* You feel sad, guilty and even angry with your little animal because he has abandoned you.

5. Your parents explain to you that your beloved hamster has died, they console you and show their support, they listen to your doubts and your questions, they answer those they can with tact and sincerity, they ask you if you want to bury your friend or say goodbye to him somehow. They accompany and support you at that time. They tell you that you can talk about it as long as you remember it. You spend a few weeks sad; you can cry and express your feelings and your parents understand it. Sometime later, your mother tells you that, if you want, you can have a parakeet or another hamster; she explains that he will have another name and he will be a different animal. You have learned something about death, about life and about your own feelings and emotions. Tomorrow the child will not remember it as traumatic and he will surely be very grateful to his parents for their tact and sincerity.

As we have mentioned, helping a child to overcome grief does not differ from helping an adult; understanding, a safe environment where the little one can feel free to ask or express his feelings, accompany, listen... For children in grief, adults are a reference, not because of what we say but because of what we do. Let us remember that we are animals who learn by imitation. If you tell your child that it is good to cry, but you hide so that he does not see a tear of yours, you are not sending the right message. It´s also not good for your child to see you at the worst moment or having a reaction of a lot of pain, because he can be scared. The best thing for him will be to see his parents or attachment figures as people who suffer like him with the loss, who express their emotions, but always within a measure, a control. He will learn from you and from this experience to manage future losses, so show him that it´s serious and that it´s sad, but that together you can overcome it. That he can cry and that he can count on you to tell you how he is doing at all times, because you are going to support him and understand him.

When we had to euthanize both Galo and Minnie, my son was not present, there were moments of so much pain that escaped my control. After a while, more appeased, we went to him and explained what had happened, in the case of Minnie, because with Galo, my son was too small. We told him that she had died, that she would no longer be home, but that she would always remain in our hearts, that the vets had tried to save her, but she was very ill. The three of us cried together and told her that we would always remember her and talk about her. A few days later we recovered her ashes, we explained to him that a part of our dog was inside that box and that the other part was in another place far superior to this one. Of course, with children it´s not as easy as a simple chat. Months later, he kept asking about her from time to time, if she lives with another family, where is she, why did she die... With a lot of patience and affection, we always answer the same thing, she is dead, she does not live here or anywhere else, because her body is gone, but she is still with us inside our hearts and when we think of her.

One of the most difficult moments in this journey is precisely the moment of giving the news to the child that the animal in the house has died. It´s very hard to have to face his reactions, his tears or his questions, but remember that it´s a very important moment, since, communicated in a wrong way, it can prolong the period of mourning. The best thing, always, will be that the person who gives the news is an attachment figure or very close to the child, that it is in a calm and safe environment, where the child feels that they can speak and ask their doubts and that they receive understanding and empathy. It´s not a good idea to postpone this moment too long, because children are very sensitive and will perceive that something is happening, they should not feel that we are excluding them from something so important; that´s why it´s good that, if they feel like it, they can participate in the rituals that are celebrated in memory of our furry companion; if we have said that it´s healing and necessary to perform a ritual or ceremony to say goodbye to our friend, why are we going to exclude children and separate them from something that is beneficial?

Let's look at the differences by age for children's grief:

- 0-2 years. At this stage, there is a total misunderstanding of the fact itself. The child has not yet developed a thought or language that allows understanding. Children will be susceptible, basically, to changes in their routines.

- 3-5 years. At this age, children still do not understand that death is irreversible. Children think that being dead is simply standing still with your eyes closed. It´s a very curious stage, so the children will ask many questions, some as absurd as: *"What do the dead eat? Will he/she be cold? When are he/she going to stop being dead and come back home? Where does he/she live now?"*. Faced with this avalanche of doubts, what we must do is to be honest and, with great tact and patience, answer their questions, over and over again, repeating the same thing. Contrary to what has been done years ago, it is inadvisable to use metaphors about death, such as saying that the dead person is asleep or that he has gone on a trip. Children may be afraid of bedtime or when a family member goes on a trip, as they will think it´s related to death. Let us remember that the child will not understand metaphors, but will take things literally. The best way to break the news to the child is for one of their support figures to accompany them to a known quiet place and to explicitly tell them that something very sad has happened, because their pet has died and he will no longer be with us; we must make it clear that it´s irreversible and that the animal will never come back, in order to not create false expectations that, in the end, will do more harm to the child. Remember that children are very self-centered, so they may think that somehow the death of their friend may be their fault. We must be on the watch with this and exonerate them at all times. Books are a good tool to explain death to a child, in a simple way. For this reason, you will find some in the bibliography of this book, which may help to put possible words that we are missing to deal with death, as well as to put images in those thoughts that children do not understand. But, above all, remember that we must explain death sincerely, without metaphors and with its consequences, from the first moment. The behaviors of children at this age when faced with a death are usually: sadness, anger, fear, worry, regression to previous behaviors, crying and tantrums.

- 6-9 years. From this age on, children develop a more realistic concept of death. The little ones already have a much more complex vocabulary, which helps them to better understand what is going on in the world. They show great interest in the details of death and, given the opportunity, at this age often want to participate in the rituals and farewell ceremonies. It´s very important that they are explained in advance how it´s going to be, what is going to happen and what is expected of them. If they want, they can read a letter, sing a song, or draw a picture for their furry friend. An adult should be by his side during the ceremony to answer all the questions that may arise, making him feel supported and listened to, but above all, included in the family, instead of being separated as it´s usually done when considering that we save them suffering, when the reality is that we deny them the learning that death is something natural and that it must be faced. If we do not know how to answer any of their questions, it´s best to be honest and tell them clearly that we do not know the answer, that there are things that no one understands. We will remember funny anecdotes about our furry, we will talk with the child about the things they did together and how much they loved each other and we will try to keep the little one with a good memory of the relationship.

Children at this age have a fear of the unknown of death, which they associate with ghosts, skeletons or other entities, and fear of separation from the family, expressing it through irritability, guilt, denial, anger, isolation, regression to previous behaviors and concentration problems in school.

- 10-13 years. At this stage, children are already aware of the irreversibility of death. They understand it´s something permanent and inevitable. They understand that all living things die at some point (including themselves), leading to greater fear of it. In this pre-adolescent age, children tend to hide their feelings more, replacing them with rebellion. They already have more abstract and spiritual thoughts about life and death. It´s important that adults act as a role model for children to grieve, in a way that helps them understand and accept their feelings. If necessary, they will help them put into words what they feel, they will be careful to give them both periods of acceptance and others of distraction. The behaviors that they can show when faced with loss at this age are usually anger, guilt, resentment, numbness, anxiety, fear of death, changes in sleep and poor school performance.

Dr. Elisabeth Kübler-Ross, of whom we have already spoken before, always carried a silkworm to funerals where children were to attend. She showed them the caterpillar and told them that it was a beautiful butterfly capable of flight, trapped in the caterpillar's wrapper, just as we are souls and energy, trapped in a physical body. The somewhat skeptical children took the caterpillar home and took care of it, until one day only an inert chrysalis appeared, the caterpillar had died. The children felt very sad but she told them that they should continue to keep the caterpillar, to see what happened after its death. One magical day, the astonished children saw the butterfly come out of them; they understood everything. The death of the caterpillar was not the end, only the transformation of the butterfly, just as the death of our physical body is not the end, but our passage to another level, where our soul and that of the beings we love has detached from its carcass, to fly in its true form. Remember: we are butterflies, we are souls.

"If there ever comes a day when we can't be together, keep me in your heart. I'm going to stay there forever..."
(Winnie the Pooh)

8. Getting out of the maze

As we have seen, grief is a process. I would say that it´s like a labyrinth full of different paths and emotions, which can make us feel confused and lost. We must allow ourselves to live it, grow and learn from it, because it can cause an introspection that will teach you to live, not only outwards, but also inwards. You have to give yourself permission to feel the full spectrum of emotions that will haunt you during this stage.

There are some myths that we have internalized, thinking that they are absolute truths, because they have usually been instilled in us as children and are socially accepted. One of them is that expressing your pain hurts yourself or others; however, it has been demonstrated that crying generates anti-stress hormones, it´s a natural relaxant and it has no side effects. Another false belief is that pain should be expressed alone, especially if you are the man of the house, but remember that we all need to express our pain, regardless of gender. In addition, all that this nonsense does is separate the home´s unity, since for other family members it can be interpreted as indifference, lack of love for the furry in the house or coldness on the part of the person who does not show feelings. We cannot teach our children that it´s good to express what we feel, if we hide it. We learn what we see, not what we hear or what we are told. It seems to us that helping is to show that nothing has happened, that pain does not exist if we do not talk about it, but that´s not true, it´s quite the opposite! The problems, the difficulties of life must be faced head-on. Pain grows in the loneliness of isolated people.

Next, we are going to see some activities that are advisable to help people after the death of their furry. Remember that there is no magic recipe that works for everyone; look for the one that is most appropriate, what catches your attention or, why not?, try each one of them, maybe the one you least imagine will help you. We can surprise ourselves; perhaps you have a talent for writing, painting or crafts, but you don't know it yet because you've never tried it. Please commit yourself and do your part, make the effort to carry them out and take the opportunity they offer you to give yourself relief and rest.

- Share your feelings. Abandon yourself to pain, alleviate it, cry, share. Give voice to the darkest thoughts that you keep in the depths of your mind, to the politically incorrect ones, share them with people who do not judge you, who listen to you and support you. Empty yourself of everything, break the wall that many times we build around us; even though they are horrible thoughts, by naming and sharing them they lose a great part of the power they have in us. Sometimes, certain traumatic moments, such as euthanizing our partner, can produce such an emotional load on our brain that we feel like it´s impossible to talk about it: we don't want to remember it, we don't even want to think about it; however, it has been shown that when we remember a difficult event and put words to describe it, being able to relive it with someone who supports us, it no longer hurts so much. Furthermore, the more you talk about the fact, paradoxically, in the long term, the less damage it will do to you. Drain yourself, underneath all that pain is you. Remember that all people are not the same and surely in your family and your circle of friends there will be different personalities. Think about each one before calling. If you want to vent, call the sensitive person, the one that you know that will listen and understand you; if you need to cheer up and think about something else, call that fun friend. Remember to ask each one what each one can give, because if you call the prankster and joker person when you need to cry and vent, he may not know how to understand your needs and you will be disappointed. Choose 4 or 5 people and write next to their name when you will call each one (distraction, walking, crying, understanding, laughing...). Do not be afraid to tell others what you need at all times.

- Write. You can keep a journal or just a few notes. Writing can help you a lot to get to know yourself. When writing, you have to name the emotions and feelings that are within you, it forces you to stop and look within; you can come out of the chaos by putting everything on paper and feel less lost; later, you can reread your writings, see everything in perspective, weigh up whether you improve or how you are evolving. Don't push away your memories or fears, express them. In my case, it helps me a lot to practice automatic writing; I relax and disconnect my mind for about 5 minutes and then I start to write down the first things that come to my mind, without thinking about them, it´s like an emptying. I take everything out and write it down on the paper, and then the mind rests. Sometimes I just write about what I would like to achieve; others, about what I don't want in my life; others, on superficial things. The important thing is not to judge yourself and to do it constantly; perhaps the first few times you don't know what to write, but you will see that little by little it will get easier. You will be able to empty the load that you carry and, including, you will be surprised by writing things that you did not know were inside you. Seriously, writing heals.

- Take care of our health. Eating well, even if we don't feel like it, is important because we are in bad enough spirits to add to that other health problems. Whether your stomach closes up or you're very hungry from anxiety, try eating healthy and nourishing things. Also, try to sleep and rest as well as possible. I know that insomnia is something natural in this phase, but we must try to combat it within our possibilities. Do not take excitements like caffeine and try to take a hot bath and relax before going to sleep. Exercise can be a good way to get tired, to produce serotonin, which is the wellness hormone, and to sunbathe, a great antidepressant. Another thing that works very well is distraction, not thinking about not being able to sleep, but taking an infusion, relaxing a little and getting into bed thinking about something else. A YouTube channel called JC2- José Carlos Carrasco has worked a lot for me. For me, he is already "my sleeping friend", because in his super-relaxing audios he helps you fall asleep, talking to you about other topics, using the technique of distraction and the truth that his talks are so interesting that it even makes me angry to fall asleep. If you think that insomnia or anxiety are out of your control, go to a specialist such as your family doctor or psychologist.

- Meditation. I think only people who meditate know the power of this activity. Something as natural as breathing can cause an anxiety attack to suddenly subside; although, well, this is not achieved just by breathing, but by breathing well. Diaphragmatic breathing has many advantages, but the most important for us are both fighting anxiety and nervousness, such as helping us focus and rest our mind. To practice it you must lie on your back, in a comfortable and relaxed place, put your hands on your abdomen and thoroughly expel the air from your lungs, even when you think you have exhaled everything, continue a little longer; once they are completely empty, inhale the air directing it to your abdomen, so that the belly swells with air, with your hands on it; hold the air for about 5 seconds, but without forcing or pressing yourself, and when you release it, do it gently through your mouth, letting your abdomen relax and your hands go down with it; stay for a moment with your lungs empty, feeling yourself relaxed and, as soon as you feel the urge to breathe in again, do it deeply and slowly, filling your lungs again, while your abdomen rises. When we concentrate on our breathing, we are aware of the here and now, we can connect with our true self. Let me tell you something that not many people know; you are not your mind, you are not your thoughts nor your emotions. You are something else. When you learn to distance yourself from those parts of your interior, when you learn to dissociate yourself from them and silence that chatter that many people have in their heads and which is called internal dialogue, you can connect with your true self; behind all that mental and emotional noise... there´s you. We think and feel so much that we often lose ourselves. Mindfulness, being present, makes us see what we are; live without the attachment of the past or the uncertainty of the future.

- Activities or hobbies. Another good way to calm your mind, without practicing meditation, is to do some activity that forces us to be focused. The important thing is to get your internal dialogue to stop and to be simply in the present moment. It can be gardening, running, furniture restoration, sewing... the important thing is to give yourself a break from your thoughts and emotions; you need to disconnect and stop thinking for a few hours.

Other activities that can help a lot are those related to art: music, drawing or writing poetry, as they can help us express things that we are not able to express with words. More and more people are able to rest their minds thanks to mandala coloring. Creativity is healing, try it!

- Volunteering. Some grieving people may miss contact with animals; however, they are not yet ready to expand the family. Volunteering with a shelter or association can be a way to help us overcome the melancholy. Being close to the reality of abandoned animals can make us see everything in perspective, contextualize and even compare these circumstances with those that our friend has had. He will surely be eternally grateful for the life he has had by your side. I know this is not going to minimize your pain, but perhaps it can expand your mind and feel that your suffering can be a path that brings you closer to others. Remember that when we give our help to others, deep down we not only help others, but they are, in turn, helping us. So, in this situation we all win; you will be in contact with the animals, you will be distracted and you will feel great and useful and the shelters will have the contribution they so badly need.

- Gratitude. Saying thank you seems very simple; however, several studies have shown the incredible power that such a simple habit can have in your day-to-day life. Gratitude is one of the most powerful feelings you can use to attract well-being. No matter who you are or where you are, gratitude has the power to remove all kinds of negativity from your life. Albert Einstein demonstrated that the universe is energy and, therefore, living beings are also energy, vibrating at different frequencies. Gratitude raises our vibrational frequency and practicing it places us on our axis. Gratitude - the more you cultivate it, the more it grows; it raises our self-esteem, makes us feel positive emotions, keeps us away from "terribilism" because it makes us more impartial and it makes us see that we always have something to be thankful for, fight depression and anxiety, beautify life and our world. To gain the habit of expressing your gratitude, there are several techniques. I'm going to explain two, but you can look for many more. On the one hand, there is the stone of gratitude; it´s simply a matter of looking for a stone that is beautiful or that catches your attention -I brought mine from the Italian coast - and put it somewhere visible or where you can you feel it. There are people who leave it on the bedside table, where they put the keys when they get home, or even carry it in their coat pocket. It consists in, every time you see or touch it, giving thanks for something; like that, several times a day. Another technique is to write or recite every morning or night (but make the routine always at the same time) and say three thanks; one addressed to you, another to someone else and the third to the world in general. Once you have the habit of giving thanks, you will no longer need anything, I assure you that it will become something innate in you.

Perhaps you are reading this chapter because you would like to help someone who is grieving for their furry. I know it can be a difficult situation where you don't really know what to say or how to act. You must know that the most important thing you can do for him, the greatest help, is simply to be there, to accompany him with love, understanding and respect. Simply letting the person express his feelings; being close to him while he cries is already helpful. It's not necessary to speak, but simply to listen. Get excited with him or hug him quietly. People who have a sympathetic friend by their side and who can vent during grief, recover better and in less time than those who do not have that help. Let your friend feel that he can get everything out of his interior, never ask him to hold back, let's make our friendship a relationship in which we can express both joy and sadness and despair.

Expressing emotions, despite the fact that many people may think otherwise, is for really strong and brave people, because you are showing your vulnerability in the eyes of others; I think there are not many things to admire so much as exposing yourself to others, that´s proving true confidence in yourself. If, on the other hand, the person you are trying to help does not open up at this moment, you should not force them. Everyone has their times and there are people who are not yet ready to express their affliction in words; in those moments, we will simply be there by his side, to walk, be silent or even talk about something else to distract him, although having a good grief means that, sooner or later, he will have to verbalize his feelings and share them with someone else. To help your friend, avoid by all means conversations related to negative things such as violence, suffering, catastrophes... on the contrary, always try to focus on positive things, create a climate of pleasant relaxation and softness, even with music. Try to propose activities that can help him, such as writing a small book about his furry's most fun anecdotes, a memorial book, going for a walk together or a walk on the beach or in the mountains, helping him save or donate the belongings of his deceased companion...

It´s very important that we normalize the situation our friend is experiencing, to make him see that he is not crazy and that all the things he feels and suffers are common in this phase. Nor should we underestimate the suffering of each person, remember that it´s an issue that causes a lot of misunderstanding in our society these days, so let's try not to criticize the person who is grieving for his animal. Do not try to impose time limits, do not set deadlines; first, he must express all his pain, cry all his tears, and once he has emotionally emptied himself of his suffering, he will begin to get up. Remember that accompanying a person in grief is not being present just for the first week or the first fifteen days, which most people usually do. To be present in the grief process is to walk this path, accompanying our friend throughout its elaboration, which, as we have already seen, is usually around a year.

Some words that can help a person in mourning are:

"I am very sorry for what you are going through. I have no words to express how I feel, I have thought about you all these days. Call me if you need to speak to someone. You will surely miss him a lot. Count on me for anything you need. People do not imagine how difficult it can be to lose an animal, even if a week has passed, it is still very difficult; I can tell our friends to contact you if you want. I will always remember him. Surely people have a hard time understanding what you are going through. Can I come by to see you in a few days? If you don't call me, can I call you? How do you feel? Do you feel like talking? Do you want us to talk about him?".

Words and phrases to avoid:

"Think it could have been worse. Don't cry anymore, it's bad for you, you'll see how time heals everything. It is the law of life. It was the best thing that could happen. Better now than within a time. You should go out more, it would do you good. Now you must think about your children and smile, it has been a long time, you shouldn't be like that, it was just an animal. If you suffer like this for an animal, I don't know what will happen when someone important dies. Don't be so over the top. Don't be so dramatic, at the end of the day it's just a dog / cat, now you have to be strong (mostly said to a child). *In time you will forget it, you will surely get over it, in a couple of weeks you will be fine. Don't worry, buy another animal just like it. Do not cry about this, it is not so bad. Life is so. You seem to care more for an animal than for people. That's just the way it is. If a week ago you were better, it seems that you are going backwards. Don't worry, children will forget, we all have to die. It is time for you to move on, to feel better and to pretend nothing had happened. It was his turn. Better not to tell him, he doesn't understand a thing anyway"* (referring to elderly people or children who lived with the animal).

As we have seen, the grieving process looks like a maze; you will have to travel many paths, some inward and some outward. There will be uphill trails that you will feel like it takes a lot of effort to advance and others downhill, through which you will run. There will be wide paths where the sun will come and you will walk accompanied by friends or family and others so narrow and dark where you will find yourself completely alone. You will get lost at its crossroads and sometimes you will come to dead ends that will make you go backwards. The incredible thing is that when you get out of the maze, you will look up, take a deep breath and observe your surroundings with new eyes. You will discover beauty in the simplest things in life that fill our days with meaning. You will be able to look up at the sky, open your arms and thank from the bottom of your heart for having shared your days with that special being, because after the pain, the tears, the anguish and the agony of detachment, you will finally be able to feel your animal within you; you will know that, as long as you live, he will be in you forever, in your memories, your anecdotes. That is the new wisdom, that is your learning. You are stronger than before and, even, you love your animal more, you have relocated him in your life, he has his place. We discover that our capacity to love remains intact or has even grown. We know what is truly important in life and that, even if another bump makes us stumble, we will have the necessary tools to overcome it. You are strong, you are love, you are resilience. You discover that, despite the pain, your heart has not dried up, but has grown so big that you have the entire universe in it.

"What we have once enjoyed and deeply loved we can never lose, for all that we love deeply becomes a part of us".
(Hellen Keller)

"We find many things in this long, strange trip sometimes, as we contemplate life, but basically we find ourselves. Who we really are, what we care about most".
(Elisabeth Kübler-Ross)

9. Life flows

When your friend leaves, it´s very understandable that you get the sensation of isolation, of not wanting to go through the same thing again and the well-known phrase appears in your mind: "I will never have another furry again". You believe that you will never feel that special connection with another being, that life will never shine again as before, that it´s impossible to regain joy and that you do not have any hope.

Although it´s totally understandable to feel like this in those moments of pain, in which you think that nothing compensates you for this suffering, that you are not a person trained to have animals because you suffer too much, that no other animal can replace your best friend and that you will never again experience as much love as you felt for him, I have to ask you to give yourself time, please reconsider, NEVER say never.

It is completely normal that during the period of grief or mourning the idea of sharing your life with another animal again doesn´t even cross your mind; what is more, I strongly ask you to never bring another animal into the house when the mourning process is still being overcome, especially if that animal is of the same species, of the same breed or physically similar to the animal that has left us... You are not going to replace your friend with another, because each animal is irreplaceable, you should not drown the sorrow for your furry by replacing it immediately; as we have seen in the chapter on grief in children, it´s not a good life lesson for them or for you. It´s a form of avoidance, so you will only be hiding your pain without having overcome it and, sooner or later, it will resurface again.

Once the mourning period has been correctly elaborated, we feel hopeful, we know that we are still capable of loving and giving love, we have emotionally relocated our animal and we know that no one else will be able to replace it; we feel stronger after we have acquired tools to manage our pain, we know ourselves better, we have learned a great lesson and we feel ready to reopen our hearts.

Depending on each person and each situation, I ask you to consider the possibility of having a new animal with you, once you feel ready. Those of us who love animals are a different species, with a giant heart and empathy, we enjoy life with them more than life without them and you must be that kind of person, otherwise, you would not have this book in your hands. We love being with them, it makes us happy to share our life with the animals and yes, we suffer when they leave, but honestly, putting everything we receive from them on a scale, **is worth it.**

Do not deny it, do not close yourself to this possibility; the possibility of continuing to share your life with an animal, especially when there are so many who need it. What do you think your friend would think? Don't you think he'd be happy that another furry in need found a home with you?

The only thing necessary to reopen your home to a new member is to have overcome the grieving process. It does not mean that you no longer remember your friend or that you do not continue crying when you see his photos, what I mean is that you have already assimilated the loss and you are not going to look for a replacement in another animal, but you are going to open the doors of your heart to another furry companion, both for him (giving an animal a good home, if it´s one of those that really need it, the better) and for yourself (enjoying games again, walks, company...).

Do not delay this phase or decision uselessly. When you feel ready, just do it. A person that opens his home again for a pet after a year doesn´t love more his buddy than a person that reopens his home after three months;

they simply have different times, but you have to know that love is not measured that way. There are people who impose themselves a certain period; this is totally insane, since we are not talking about something measurable. In this case, the important thing is to have left the maze. Let us remember that a person who suffers a chronic grief will take more than two years to be ready to welcome a new furry, while a resilient person can be ready in just a few months.

Personally, I will always recommend the adoption of an animal that is suffering in a cage. Let us remember that in our country (Spain in this case) there is a very high dropout rate, compared to the other countries of the European Union. It´s indescribable the feeling of adopting an animal that really needs it. Currently, the associations and shelters in Spain are overwhelmed to such an extent that they have to send animals to adopt to other European countries. If you like a particular breed of dog or cat (although I must confess that, for me, the mixed-races are the best breed, the healthiest, the smartest and all loving), there are many associations that are in charge of giving animals of specific breed for adoption, such as Galgos del Sur, Galgos 112, Nórdicos en adopción, Agranda for German Bulldogs and big dogs, Sos Golden, Adopciones exóticos, Sos Yorkshire, among others. It´s true that in many of these cases, the animals that are in these associations will not only be puppies, it´s possible they are young animals and it may be that they are adult cats and dogs. Remember that, normally, they are puppies bought when they are about three months old and that when they grow up, they end up in one of these associations, when their owners realize that the animal is no longer so cute, that they cannot go on vacation or that it sucks having to take him out for a walk every day. I encourage you to consider the option of adopting an adult companion and I will just list some of the advantages that it has over a puppy: you don´t have to teach him to do his needs outside, since many have already learned it and you won't need to spend all day picking up pee and poop from your house; they already have the vast majority of vaccines, so you won't have to keep him locked up at home without going out until he's got them all; many associations deliver them already sterilized, so you will save yourself many health and behavioral problems in the future; they are a bit past the age of playing pranks, so they are less likely to bite your furniture when their teeth are changing; you know in advance what character he will have, if he is nervous or calm, if he likes children or not, among other things. Depending on what you are looking for and depending on your lifestyle, the balance will weigh more to one side or the other. All I ask of you is that, evaluating your level of time, involvement and your rhythm of life, you contemplate the two possibilities, but do not immediately dismiss the option of adopting an adult, because I can assure you from my experience with Minnie, that the furry is going to get used to you and to your house even if you have not raised him since he was a puppy; what's more, he will be super grateful because he will have suffered a lot in his life or... why not?, even adopt a senior buddy. What greater gift could you give to an animal that has waited all its life for a home in the solitude of a shelter, than to welcome him during his last years and make them the best?

I repeat, do not impose on yourself a certain time or a certain type of friend. You simply have to let events flow and when the right time comes, make the decision. When you have doubts about this or any other dilemma in your life, I propose a simple question that a very special person, named Lucia, taught me and that has meant a before and an after in my life: always ask yourself from what type of feeling are you choosing; from love or from fear? They are usually the two main emotions in our life, so it´s in your hand to follow the path of love and abundance or that of fear and scarcity. If we make our decision from fear (suffering, seeing ourselves alone, leaving our comfort zone, limiting beliefs with which we live, scarcity...), normally, they are responses that our mind dictates and that is not usually what we really want, but what we think we have to do. On the contrary, we can make our decision from love (to ourselves, to others, to compassion, to the truth, to our inspiration...); normally, they are answers that our soul dictates, our intuition, that it´s nothing other than our true self, away from our controlling mind. So, if your main reason for adopting an animal, being in a relationship or continuing with your job is fear, in any of its variants, I recommend that you let it be. If your main reason for any of the previous examples is love or any of its variants, such as compassion, the desire to share or self-fulfillment... Go ahead! You are choosing from the correct emotion, which will lead your life to that path and you will live from your true self.

Remember, your capacity to love continues intact within you. I assure you that you will love again with the same intensity, that you will laugh again, that you will enjoy again, that you will once again share your life with an incredible furry, with whom you will have a great connection, but above all, I assure you that it will be worth it.

"There is no greater act of compassion than to give heaven to those who have lived in hell".
(Unknown)

"If we never experience the chill of a dark winter, it is very unlikely that we will ever cherish the warmth of a bright summer's day. Nothing stimulates our appetite for the simple joys of life more than the starvation caused by sadness or desperation. In order to complete our amazing life journey successfully, it is vital that we return each dark tear in a pearl of wisdom, and find the blessing in each curse".
(Anthon St. Maarten)

10. The legend of the Rainbow Bridge

As the story of the Rainbow Bridge goes, when the four-legged angels (and any other creature that we have loved) say goodbye to us and with a sigh they let out their last goodbye, they cross this bridge. On the other side of this, there are meadows and hills, where they can run, play and enjoy their innocence...

Legend has it that on the other side of the Rainbow Bridge, there is enough space, food, water and sun for all of them to feel good. Furthermore, according to this legend, all those who have been sick, mutilated or cruelly injured, see their health restored and overflow with joy.

In line with this beautiful legend, our friends are happy and satisfied, except that they miss someone special that they left on the other side of the Rainbow Bridge. So, all of a sudden, while everyone is running around and playing, one of them stops and stares with his sparkling eyes at the horizon. His body shudders and with great excitement he separates from his group, running fast across the field. They see us in the middle of the bridge and run quickly to welcome us. According to the legend of the Rainbow Bridge, in that moment humans and animals, friends of the soul, get together and never ever get separated.

His wet licks bathe our face and our hands cannot help but caress our four-legged angel, our beloved creature. Then, in line with the legend, we remain united throughout eternity, through a mutual and wise look, full of love and nobility.

But here, far from ending the legend, it continues...

Suddenly, on the Rainbow Bridge, the morning dawned differently from normal days, so full of sun; this was a cold and gray day, the saddest day you can imagine. The newcomers did not know what to think, they had never seen such a day there. But the animals that had been waiting the longest for their loved ones knew exactly what was going on and gathered on the path that leads to the bridge to watch.

They waited a bit and a very old animal arrived, with his lowered head and dragging his tail. The animals that had been there for a long time knew immediately what his story was, because they had seen this happen many times. This little animal was approaching slowly, very slowly, it was obvious that he was in great emotional pain, although there were no physical signs of pain.

Unlike the other animals waiting in the bridge, this animal had not returned to youth nor had returned to being full of health and joy. As he walked to the bridge, he saw how all the other animals were looking at him. He knew that this was not his place and that the sooner he could cross the bridge, he would be happy. But this would not be so. When he approached the bridge, an angel appeared and, with a sad face, asked him for forgiveness and told him that he could not cross. Only those animals that were accompanied by their loved ones could cross the Rainbow Bridge. With nowhere else to go, the older animal turned around and, among the meadows, he saw a group of other animals like himself, some older, others very fragile. They weren't playing games, they were just lying in the grass, looking at the path that led to the Rainbow Bridge. So, he went to join them, looking at the road and stood there, waiting.

"Do you see that poor animal and the others who are there with him?" They are the animals that never had a person. This, at least, reached a refuge; entered it, just as you see it now, an older animal, with gray hair and somewhat cloudy eyesight. But he never managed to leave the shelter and he died only with the affection of his caretaker, to accompany him while he left Earth. Since he did not have a family to give him his love, he has no one to accompany him across the bridge."

The first animal thought for a moment and he asked:

"And what will happen now?"

Before receiving the answer, clouds began to break and a very strong wind made them disappear. They could see a person, alone, approaching the bridge, and among the older animals, a whole group of them was suddenly bathed in a golden light and again they were young and healthy animals, full of life.

"Look and you will know", said the second one.

Another group of animals that have been waiting also approached the road and lowered their heads, while that person approached. Passing in front of each head, the person touched each one; to some of them he gave a caress, to others he scratched their ears affectionately... The rejuvenated animals lined up behind and followed the person to the bridge. Then, they crossed the Rainbow Bridge together.

"What was that?" asked the first animal. And the second one he said:

"That person was a rescuer, a great lover of animals and worked in their defense. The animals that you saw lowering their heads, as a sign of respect, were those that were saved thanks to the efforts of such people, and those that you saw older and then rejuvenated, were those that never found a home… and since they had no family, they couldn't cross the bridge. When a person who has worked on Earth to help abandoned animals arrives, they are allowed one last act of rescue and love. All those poor animals for whom they could not find families on Earth are allowed to accompany them so that they can also cross the Rainbow Bridge".

This legend is anonymous.

Thanks to all those angels on Earth, dedicated body and soul to help abandoned animals. Not only you make this world a better place, but you illuminate the true essence of the human being and elevate our species to the highest level, showing the way to goodness and love.

11. Open your heart

As you can see throughout all these pages, you have a very personal book in your hands; I do not believe that someone´s heart can be reached if we do not open ours first. In each letter that I have written, I have uncovered my soul, my sufferings, my happy memories and the most painful ones. I have cried and laughed writing this book, I have tried to give practical information about grief, but also spiritual. I have encouraged you to do some introspection work while I myself was doing it and I can say that writing this book has healed me, as I hope it can help you heal as well, so after sharing so much, I felt in debt to tell how my story ends.

After the death of Minnie, which due to the circumstances was terribly painful since we were practically all day together and she suddenly left us because of an unexpected illness, I began to write this book.

I continued to share my life with my animals, our kitten Deysi and Lolita, our Amazon parrot and, without a doubt, the leader of the pack. When I least expected it, while I was putting the finishing touches on the book, and thanks to my husband, Oreo, an adopted greyhound, came home.

Oreo was something unexpected for me and I'm going to share a secret with you: Oreo is everything I didn't want, at that moment, in a dog. Do you remember when we talked about opening our hearts and not setting limits? Well, I spoke knowingly. I did not want to have a dog again because of the pain of the situation, but if I had made an exception, that dog would not have been black under no circumstances, since I did not want to feel that he was replacing Minnie; if he had been black, I would not have wanted him to be very old, because I did not want to go through this pain for many years from now; if he had been black and older, I would not have wanted him to be an abused dog, because I would feel that I was reliving my story; I would not have wanted for anything in the world that he had hazel eyes, that they looked at me as if I were an angel on earth... no, I would not have wanted any of that and all of that is precisely Oreo: black, with the weith of years hanging, abused, with that look. Still, I am a person who believes in the universe and I believe that both good and bad things come into my life for only one reason: lessons. And I try to take notes and learn from all of them. So... I got it, destiny, I don't have to set limits, I don't have to judge myself or others and I have to let everything flow. Yes, Oreo is everything my narrow mind didn't want in a dog, but he's everything my newly recovered heart needed.

How can I not feel connection, when my wounded soul contemplates his completely scarred body? How can I not want to feed that being, when my fingers caress that skin and bones body? How can I not want to offer the warmth of my home to those who have their whole body covered with calluses from sleeping on the hard and cold floor? How could I not love someone who only needed a caress, to follow us from the first day throughout the house, afraid of losing one of the few people who had shown him affection? He is obedient from day one, smart, loving, patient, calm... Why had my mind put such absurd prejudices inside my head? What can the color of an animal or its eyes matter, when what it is about, what it has always been about, is about the soul? Oreo doesn't look like an abused dog, even if his body says otherwise. He has love for everyone, without resentment, without distrust, giving a second chance to the species that has reduced him to the state he was in. He only needs a couple of caresses and a corner in my living room and he has already given us his heart. Can there be a soul purer than that of animals? I find it hard to believe.

Reopening your life and your home to another animal, after the loss, is like falling in love again after your heart has been broken. A brave and crazy gesture that makes you enjoy everything, even more than the first time. You know where you are heading to and that is why you are willing to enjoy it with your whole being, to live each moment and give as much love as possible. I know that I will return to the labyrinth, sooner or later, but I also know that this is a sign that I am still here, that I continue to love; my heart has not dried up; on the contrary, thanks to my boys who left, now it is bigger and stronger. Able to love once more, able to see a soul behind a wet snout. I feel that I can harbor the love of each one of them in me and continue adding. Welcome to our heart forever, Oreo!

Oreo was abandoned by a hunter, along with 13 other greyhounds, in the Sadeco shelter, in Córdoba, in what is called "discard", at the end of the hunting season.

His former owner did not know how to see the wonderful being he had before him. The Galgos del Sur Association saved them all and kept them in their shelter, while they found family.

"Until one has loved an animal, a part of one's soul remains unawakened".
(Anatole France)

"Since compassion for animals is so intimately associated with goodness of character, it may be confidently asserted that whoever is cruel to animals cannot be a good man. Boundless compassion for all living beings is the firmest and surest guarantee of pure moral conduct".
(Arthur Schopenhauer)

Words for Minnie

In 2009, I met by chance some girls from an animal shelter and I decided to collaborate with them, helping with promotion tasks. Then I saw a cruel reality that I had never been aware of: the number of abandoned animals in the world. At home, we had always bought the dogs that had lived with us and my first dog, after I became independent, was also bought; so, I decided to give him a sister and without thinking I went to the municipal shelter of Cagliari, where I lived at that time, and I told the boy who was there:

"I'm coming for the worst dog you have".

Imagine the face that the poor boy had, but I insisted:

"I come for the dog that no one would ever take".

After the initial surprise, he accompanied me through corridors full of puppies, young and purebred dogs, then by very cute mixed-breed with soft hair and cinnamon colors, until we reached the last cage in the last corridor and he pointed at *her*.

"This dog shouldn't even be here", he told me.

He explained that they had so many dogs that only those with the best chance of being adopted lived in the city shelter; the others lived in other facilities, in the mountains. In Italy, unlike Spain, they follow a o-slaughter policy, which means that they do not put down animals in the shelters after x days or months, they keep them forever.

He told me that she had only been brought from the mountain because she had been sterilized and the vet had to see her because of the stitches.

"This is the worst", he told me, "she is black, middle race, mixed-breed, mixture of PPP, she is an adult and does not allow to be touched because she is very afraid of people; we believe they used it as sparring" (training for fighting dogs); "she does not know how to walk down the street or wear a collar or strap, she has two pellet wounds in the hip, she´s just skin and bones and her belly is full of stitches".

"Okay. I'll take her".

"Are you sure? I think you should think about it on the weekend; besides, this is NOT a normal dog, you will never be able to do normal things with her: neither caress her nor take her to the park... really, I think you should think about it, we have many better dogs than her".

Now, almost 10 years later, my little girl has just left me. I just wish I could see this boy again to tell him I'm sorry, but he was completely wrong, he didn't give me the worst dog: HE GAVE ME THE BEST DOG I COULD HAVE DREAMED.

Although it took me a month to caress her, for me it was the softest touch in the world; yes, it took her six months to lick me for the first time and for me that kiss was worth a thousand given by other dogs; it took her a year to lie down to sleep with me and it was the best nap of my life; I worked a long time to get her to walk fearlessly down the street, but her walks with me were unforgettable.

She has been loving, protective, playful, calm; we have traveled half of Europe together, we have gone to dog parks, to the beach, to the snow; she has seen my life collapse and she has seen my happiness rebuild; she has been by my side while we created a family; she has had her brother Galo, whom drool she has tolerated; she has had a cat sister, Deysi, with whom she snuggled to sleep together; she has had a human brother, Neizan, to whom he has allowed everything and has loved him very much; she has had her daddy Jorge, whom she adored; she has been by my side through good and bad times, when I had no one I had her, and I can only reproach her for one thing: she has left an immense emptiness in our hearts.

Thank you for sharing so much, thank you for all the lessons you have taught me, thank you for inspiring this book. You'll be always in me.

That though the radiance which was
once so bright be now forever taken from my
sight. Though nothing can bring back the
hour of splendor in the grass, glory in the flower.
We will grieve not, rather find strength
in what remains behind".
(William Wordsworth)

(For Minnie and Luis)

Dear reader:

T hank you for coming this far, I sincerely hope that this book has helped you to go through this difficult stage of your life.

I wish that you can look at the past with gratitude instead of pain, that you live your life from love and not from fear, that this suffering does not make your heart close, but rather open to house the whole world in it. I wish that you feel that your partner is within you and that very soon you will be together again.

Thank you for having seen a soul behind a snout.

If you think that this work can help other people who are going through or are going to go through the same thing as you, I encourage you to help them find this book, leaving a comment about it or sharing it on your social networks.

If you want to know more about my services or you need help, you can find me here:

⇨ Instagram and Facebook: Espérame en el arcoíris

✉ E-mail: huellaemocional@hotmail.com

I must thank my most avid readers for their valuable advice: Rebeca, Noelia, Lidia, Laura and Sara. This book is much more beautiful thanks to you.

Also, thanks to Lucía and the girls in our support group. You are connection and light, even in the distance.

To my parents. I am what I am thanks to you.

As with all the good things I have in my life, I have to thank my husband and my son.

Thanks to all the people capable of giving and receiving love from our little brothers, the animals.

Thanks to all the furries in my life.

To those who has passed, to those who are, to those who will come.

Recommended bibliography

You may find many of these books in English, like the ones by Elisabeth Kübler-Ross, Eckhart Tole, Benji Davies, Hans Wilhelm.

La inutilidad del sufrimiento, by María Jesús Álava Reyes. La esfera de los libros.

Déjame llorar, by Anji Carmelo. Taranna Ediciones.

La rueda de la vida, by Elisabeth Kübler-Ross. Vergara Ediciones.

La muerte: un amanecer, by Elisabet Kübler-Ross. Grupo Planeta Spain.

Los niños y la muerte, by Elisabeth Kübler-Ross. Luciérnaga.

Sobre la muerte y los moribundos, by Elisabeth KüblerRoss. Ediciones de bolsillo.

El mensaje de las lágrimas, by Alba Payás Puigarnau. Paidós Divulgación.

El poder del ahora, by Eckhart Tole. Gaia.

Así es la vida, by Ana-Luisa Ramírez, Carmen Ramírez. Editorial Diálogo (children´s book).

Siempre, by Ana Galán y Marta. Sedano Ediciones Bruño (children´s book).

La isla del abuelo, by Benji Davies. Andana Edición (children´s book).

Yo siempre te querré, by Hans Wilhelm. Editorial Juventud, S.A (children´s book).

Dime quién ama de verdad, by Beret Canción.

Made in United States
Orlando, FL
31 October 2024